GW00384887

LAMENT

*Scottish poems for
funerals and consolation*

Lament

Scottish poems for funerals and consolation

Introduction by
RICHARD HOLLOWAY

Edited by
LIZZIE MACGREGOR

SCOTTISH POETRY LIBRARY
By leaves we live

Polygon

In memory of my sister

First published in 2005 by
The Scottish Poetry Library
5 Crichton's Close
Edinburgh EH8 8DT
In association with
POLYGON

ISBN 10: 1 904598 52 8
ISBN 13: 9 781904 598527

The publishers acknowledge support from
the Scottish Arts Council
towards the publication of this title

Designed and typeset in
10/14pt Foundry Sans by James Hutcheson
Printed and bound by
The Cromwell Press, Trowbridge, Wiltshire

Scottish
Arts Council
LOTTERY FUNDED

Death is the port where all may refuge finde,
The end of labour, entry unto rest . . .

From 'The Alexandrean Tragedie'
by SIR WILLIAM ALEXANDER

ACKNOWLEDGEMENTS

Our thanks are due to the following authors, publishers, and estates who have generously given permission to reproduce works:

George Mackay Brown, 'Elegy for a Child' from *Travellers: poems* (John Murray, 2001), and 'In Memoriam I.K.' from *The Wreck of the Archangel: poems* (John Murray, 1989), reprinted by permission of Archie Bevan and John Murray Ltd; George Bruce, 'Departure and Departure and ...' from *Today Tomorrow: collected poems 1933-2000* (Polygon, 2001), reprinted by permission of the George Bruce Estate; John Burnside, 'Metamorphosis' from *The Light Trap* (Jonathan Cape, 2002) reprinted by permission of The Random House Group Ltd; R.L. Cook, 'Bide Ye Wi Me' (*Lallans*, No.57, 2000) reprinted by permission of Lindsay Cook; Christine De Luca, 'A Peerie Codicil / A Little Codicil' from *Wast wi da Valkyries: poems in English and Shetland dialect* (Shetland Library, 1997), reprinted by permission of the author; Hamish Henderson, 'The Flyting o' Life and Daith' from *Collected Poems and songs* (Curly Snake Publishing, 2000), reprinted by permission of the Henderson Estate; Violet Jacob, 'The Brig' from *The Scottish Poems of Violet Jacob* (Oliver and Boyd, 1945), reprinted by permission of Malcolm Hutton; Paula Jennings, 'Walking with You' copyright © 2005, printed by permission of the author; Norman MacCaig, 'Praise of a man' from *Collected Poems* (Chatto & Windus, 1990), reprinted by permission of Polygon Ltd; Ewan MacColl, 'The Joy of Living', reprinted by permission of Harmony Music; Donald John MacDonald, 'Do Làmh a Chrìosda / Your Hand, O Christ' from *Chì Mi: bàrdachd Dhòmhnall Iain Donnchaidh / I See: the poetry of Donald John MacDonald* (Birlinn, 2001), reprinted by permission of Bill Innes; Gordon Meade, 'The Long Drive Home' from *A Man at Sea* (diehard, 2003), reprinted by permission of the author; Edwin Morgan, from 'Elegy on Jean Calvin' from *Scottish Religious Verse* (St Andrew Press, 2000), reprinted by permission of the author; Janet Paisley, 'Mountain Thyme' from *Reading the Bones* (Canongate, 1999), reprinted by permission of the author; David Purves, 'On Daith' copyright © 2005, printed by permission of the author; Kathleen Raine, 'Change' from *Collected Poems* (Golgonooza Press, 2000), reprinted by permission of Golgonooza Press; James Robertson, 'The Bird that was Trapped has Flown' copyright © 2003, reprinted by permission of the author; Robin Robertson, 'Fall' from *Slow Air* (Picador, 2002), reprinted by permission of Macmillan, London, UK; Iain Crichton Smith, 'On Looking at the Dead' from *Collected Poems* (Carcanet, 1995), reprinted by permission of Carcanet Press; Sydney Goodsir Smith, 'Hamewith' from *Collected Poems* (John Calder, 1975), reprinted by permission of Calder Publications UK; William Soutar, 'The Flourish Aye is at the Fa' from *Collected Poems* (Andrew Dakers, 1948), and 'Song' from *Poems of William Soutar: a new selection* (Scottish Academic Press, 1988), reprinted by permission of the Trustees of the National Library of Scotland; Gael Turnbull, 'For Them' copyright © 2005, printed by permission of Jill Turnbull; Hamish Whyte, 'White Wave' copyright © 2005, printed by permission of the author; Douglas Young, 'The 23rd Psalm o King Dauvit' from *A Braird o Thristles: Scots poems* (William MacLellan, 1947), reprinted by permission of Clara Young.

CONTENTS

INTRODUCTION

One of the most dramatic churches in Edinburgh is called Old St Paul's. It is built half way down one of those ribs or closes that curve down off the spine of the Royal Mile. The best way to get in is through a little door on Carrubber's Close. You duck in through the inconspicuous entrance and walk in suddenly to space and mystery. If you wander to the other end of the church, you come to a wide dramatic stairway that leads down to the official entrance in Jeffrey Street. It was down that stair that I led countless funeral processions during the twelve years I was Rector. It was part of the tradition of the place that the dead would be brought to church and lie in their coffins in the chancel the night before the funeral. At the end of the service I would lead the cortège out and down the stairs to the street below, reciting the Song of Simeon from the Gospel of Luke:

Lord now lettest thou thy servant depart in peace...

I would shiver at the solemn finality of these last journeys of earth back to earth, ashes back to ashes, dust back to dust, which are the common lot of humanity. There were times when I never wanted to do it again; times when I didn't want to lead yet another procession of mourners to the graveside; times when anger rose in me at the pointlessness of another set of shattered lives, as a young couple lamented the death of a child, or a wife the death of a husband cut down in his prime, or middle-aged men and women mourned the death of a beloved parent. But on it went, year after year, because we are all on the way to death, all old enough to die, and death is no respecter of times and seasons: it snatches us from life not when we feel ready, but when it feels like it.

So it is not surprising that over the centuries we have learned how to mark these endless processions to the grave with word and ceremony. Until fairly recently, most of these services in Scotland would have been conducted according to the liturgies of the Christian churches. They would vary according to the traditions of the denomination, but all would have had important things in common, the main one being that they would all have heard some of the great passages from the New Testament celebrating the Church's belief in the resurrection of the dead:

> *I am the resurrection and the life, saith the Lord: he that believeth in me, though he were dead, yet shall he live . . ...*
> *We shall not all sleep, but we shall all be changed, in a moment, in the twinkling of an eye, at the last trump: for the trumpet shall sound and the dead shall be raised incorruptible, and we shall be changed . . .*

Even when I was more comfortable with the idea of the resurrection of the dead than I subsequently became, I used to wonder about the moral efficacy of the Church's strong emphasis on death as the gateway to a greater life. I could see that for believers it took some of the sting out of death; but did it really let the bereaved pour out their grief at the loss they had suffered? Where was the place for passionate lament in the midst of this confident assertion that death was nothing? That was when I longed for different texts, texts that would let me express the weariness and sorrow of all this dying. And when I started doing funerals for unbelievers, for mourners who did not believe that their beloved dead had gone over to the other side to wait for them, the lack of appropriate readings and ceremonies struck me even more forcibly. What I needed then, in fact, is the exquisite little volume you hold in your hands now: *Lament: Scottish poems for funerals and consolation*.

The double purpose behind the volume suggested by the sub-title is important. When we lose someone to death there are two things we need to do, one public, the other private. We need a ceremony that, in the midst of relatives and friends, allows us to express our gratitude for the ones we have lost and mourn their passing. But we also need texts for private consolation, words that help us express and maybe even endure the sorrow we are feeling. *Lament* has texts for both purposes. There is, for instance, Gael Turnbull's remarkable threnody, 'For Them', that allows three mourners to express their grief and gratitude for those who have gone:

> for them
> > a gift
> > > before the door is shut . . .

In a different mode, there are Scots versions of famous texts traditionally used at Christian funerals, one from the Psalter, the other from the Hymn Book. 'Abide with Me' must be the number one favourite hymn at funerals, so what about using the version provided here by R. L. Cook:

> Bide ye wi me: the nicht begins to glour;
> Mirk is aa aboot me, haud me i thy pooer...

or Douglas Young's version of Psalm 23:

The Lord's my herd, I sall nocht want...

On the other hand, for the mood of quiet consolation there are some lovely poems in this little book. The most wrenching death is that of a child, caught perfectly here by George Mackay Brown's 'Elegy for a Child'. What can be said when you've lost a pal or an auld acquaintance? If he's a golfing companion, have a look at Gordon Meade's 'The Long Drive Home'. As one who fears the possibility that Scotland is being converted into a series of supermarkets spread out among coast-to-coast golf courses, I was moved by the discovery that you can even make poetry out of our national obsession with the wee white ball: but what do I know? Well, this actually: that the Scottish Poetry Library has followed its little book of poems for weddings and affirmations, *Handfast*, with another beautiful and helpful gathering of texts, abundant with consolation.

RICHARD HOLLOWAY

Change

CHANGE
Said the sun to the moon,
You cannot stay.

Change
Says moon to the waters,
All is flowing.

Change
Says the field to the grass,
Seed-time and harvest,
Chaff and grain.

You must change,
Said the worm to the bud,
Though not to a rose,

Petals fade
That wings may rise
Borne on the wind.

You are changing,
Said death to the maiden, your wan face
To memory, to beauty.

Are you ready to change?
Says thought to the heart, to let pass
All your lifelong

For the unknown, the unborn
In the alchemy
Of the world's dream?

You will change,
Say the stars to the sun,
Says night to the stars.

KATHLEEN RAINE

from **Elegy on Jean Calvin**

For the dead weight of your body with its
   apprehensions
Has left you, you are beyond the stars, you nudge
God, you enjoy the one your mind adored,
You see pure light within pure light, you drink
Divinity poured brimming into you,
Your life has become an everlasting thing
Unanxious, impervious to empty-headed joys
Or devastating fears or the hammer of grief
Or the cancer of disease creeping from body to soul.
As for me, I call that morning which released you
From bitterest cares a very birthday: snatched
To the stars, you re-entered your old homeland,
You left a repellent exile behind, your mind
Scoffs at any second death, rules the supposed
Rule of fate, steps into the vista
Of an immeasurable life.

from the Latin of GEORGE BUCHANAN (1506–1582)
translated by EDWIN MORGAN

The Flourish Aye is at the Fa'

The flourish aye is at the fa';
The bird aye blythe to be awa:
What we touch is never taen:
What we hae we canna hain.

Lichtly haud the gifted hour:
Lichtly gether and gie owre:
Life blaws in frae ilka airt:
Bigg nae wa' to hap the hert.

WILLIAM SOUTAR

fa'	*fall*
blythe	*glad*
taen	*taken*
hain	*hoard*
haud	*hold*
gie owre	*give away*
frae ilka airt	*from every direction*
bigg	*build*
wa'	*wall*
hap	*shield*

'The Heart Could Never Speak'

The heart could never speak
But that the Word was spoken.
We hear the heart break
Here with hearts unbroken.
Time, teach us the art
That breaks and heals the heart.

Heart, you would be dumb
But that your word was said
In time, and the echoes come
Thronging from the dead.
Time, teach us the art
That resurrects the heart.

Tongue, you can only say
Syllables, joy and pain,
Till time, having its way,
Makes the word live again.
Time, merciful lord,
Grant us to learn your word.

EDWIN MUIR

On Daith

Gin ye wad prie the speirit o Daith,
open wyde yeir hert in the bodie o Lyfe,
for Lyfe an Daith is aw ane, even as
the skelterin burn an the sea is aw ane ...

For whit is it ti die, but ti staun naukit
afore the wund an ti melt intil the sun?
An whit is it ti stap breathin, but ti free
the braith frae its restless tydes, sae it micht
growe foraye an seek for God unhinnert?

Anelie whan ye waucht frae the river o seilence,
sal ye trulie lilt,
an whan ye hae wun til the peak o the ferr ben,
wul ye stert ti sklim free,
an whan the yird gethers back yeir spauls,
syne, ye sal trulie daunce!

from *The Prophet* by KAHLIL GIBRAN
owreset intil Scots bi DAVID PURVES

gin	*if*
prie	*taste*
skelterin burn	*scurrying stream*
staun naukit	*stand naked*
anelie	*only*
waucht	*drink*
lilt	*sing*
ferr ben	*far mountain*
sklim	*climb*
yird	*earth*
spauls	*limbs*
syne	*then*

Elegy for a Child

This second door stood open only a short while.
Now close it gently.
The ghost has gathered its few belongings into a bag.
It has gone through the garden gate.
It has turned its back on the fire, the roses, the stories.

Fragrance from lintel and threshold –
Fragrance of bread –
Fragrance of sharing, after a good word uttered –
Fragrance of laughter too young for mockery.

Have you seen a disturbance in the blue wind
Between the cold hearth and the moor?
The brief flesh
About the bone, brighter than a cornfield
And the ghost beyond dew and snowflakes bright.

(For a short time it is lost – it weeps –
It does not know where to go.
Ears are too gross for its grief and questionings.)

Shut the door gently upon women's weeping.
Twelve hands
Light him in at the door of his first mother.

February 1983–August 1984

GEORGE MACKAY BROWN

A Peerie Codicil

Dinna lay me wi uncan fok
ta lie a thoosand year
sabbin dagidder; da stane
heavy, marking oot a piece o laand
ithoot meanin.

Slock me whick an clean:
lat da ess birl whaar hit wil:
nae monimints. A'm in dee:
an du's mi mindin.

A Little Codicil

Do not lay me between strangers
to lie a thousand years
co-mingling; the stone
heavy, marking out a territory
without meaning.

Quench me clean and quick:
let the ash fly lightly
where it will: no stone,
no plaque. I am in you:
you are my memorial.

CHRISTINE DE LUCA

Bide Ye Wi Me

Bide ye wi me: the nicht begins tae glour;
Mirk is aa aboot me, haud me i thy pooer;
Help o man it canna bide an I've nae comfort mair:
Bide ye wi me an bield me i thy care.

Life's wee bit glisk o licht sune smoors awa;
Aa the warld's swack tooers maun dirl an brak an faa:
Naething but change comes birlan tae my e'e –
Bide ye, that wullna change, richt close tae me.

I canna live withoot thy haun tae guide
Me wi the luve that blaws the deevil's pride
Aagate – whit neuk can tent me safe frae hairm
In ony weather save the crook o thine airm.

Carlins an warlocks daurna rax me there;
Aa this warld's waesome bogles are nae mair:
Whaur's the dirk o daith – Och grave thy pooer's
     a lee;
I'll thole it aa sin thou'll jist bide wi me.

Whan tae the yird I start tae shauchle doon,
Come Lord i licht tae shaw me that abune
Aa the warld's wersh an direfu' mirk I'll see
The michty ben o heaven, whaur I'll bide wi thee.

from 'Abide with Me' by HENRY F. LYTE
Scots version by R. L. COOK

mirk	*darkness*
bield	*shelter*
glisk	*glimmer*
smoors awa	*dies down*
swack tooers	*weak towers*
dirl	*shake*
birlan	*whirling*
aagate	*all over the place*
whit neuk	*which corner*
tent	*hold*
carlins	*witches*
daurna rax	*dare not reach*
thole	*bear*
yird	*earth*
shauchle	*shuffle*
wersh	*bitter*

On Looking at the Dead

This is a coming to reality.
This is the stubborn place. No metaphors swarm

around that fact, around that strangest thing,
that being that was and now no longer is.

This is a coming to a rock in space
worse than a rock (or less), diminished thing

worse and more empty than an empty vase.

The devious mind elaborates its rays.
This is the stubborn thing. It will not move.

It will not travel from our stony gaze.

But it must stay and that's the worst of it
till changed by processes. Otherwise it stays.

To beat against it and no waves of grace
ever to ascend or sovereign price

to be held above it! This is no hero. This
is an ordinary death. If there is grace

theology is distant. Sanctify
(or so they say) whatever really is

and this is real, nothing more real than this.
It beats you down to it, will not permit

the play of imagery, the peacock dance,
the bridal energy or mushrooming crown

or any blossom. It only is itself.
It isn't you. It only is itself.

It is the stubbornness of a real thing

mentionable as such and only such,
the eyes returning nothing. Compromise

is not a meaning of this universe.
And that is good. To face it where it is,

to stand against it in no middle way
but in the very centre where things are

and having it as centre, for you take
directions from it not as from a book

but from this star, black and fixed and here,
a brutal thing where no chimeras are

nor purple colours nor a gleam of silk
nor any embroideries eastern or the rest

but unavoidable beyond your choice
and therefore central and of major price.

IAIN CRICHTON SMITH

In Memoriam I. K.

That one should leave The Green Wood suddenly
    In the good comrade-time of youth,
    And clothed in the first coat of truth
Set out alone on an uncharted sea:

Who'll ever know what star
    Summoned him, what mysterious shell
    Locked in his ear that music and that spell,
And what grave ship was waiting for him there?

The greenwood empties soon of leaf and song.
    Truth turns to pain. Our coats grow sere.
    Barren the comings and goings on this shore.
He anchors off The Island of the Young.

GEORGE MACKAY BROWN

White Wave

you are scattered on the water
where rocks burn in the sun
where seals come to sing
where gannets fold and plunge
where sea-thrift keeps its hold
    in all weathers

you are the white wave
blown by the wind
you are the wind
that blows the white wave

HAMISH WHYTE

Mountain Thyme

We build a raft of heather roots
and go with you to that shore.
Wreathed in poem and song, we
thread wild thyme through your hair.

The hills, always your home,
hold steady, and proudly the pipes
announce your coming in the air.

Mouths full of ash, words done,
all that can be held now is the cord
to slip you free, and gone. We bear
the weight as you would wish us to

and pay you back into the tidal earth,
into the promise of your birth,
as you go from us. As you go.

JANET PAISLEY

Requiem

Under the wide and starry sky,
Dig the grave and let me lie.
Glad did I live and gladly die,
    And I laid me down with a will.

This be the verse you grave for me:
Here he lies where he longed to be;
Home is the sailor, home from sea,
    And the hunter home from the hill.

ROBERT LOUIS STEVENSON

For Them (A Threnody)

for them
>> a gift
>>>> before the door is shut
for them
>> a sleep
>>>> as a weight shaken off
for them
>> a word
>>>> against the mercy of time
for them
>> a memory
>>>> by chance and yet chosen
for them
>> a brightness
>>>> in the dark between the stars
for them
>> a place
>>>> through which to pass
for them
>> a voice
>>>> with no need to reply
for them
>> a time
>>>> late but no less

for them
      a silence
            beyond mere limitation
for them
      a moment
            to keep what is

GAEL TURNBULL

Note: This could be used with three voices reading in turn and introduced as 'For all who have gone before us' . . . but as might seem appropriate.

The Long Drive Home

We are born in an open field
and we die in a dark wood.

Russian proverb

One hook too many, one slice too far
has brought him out of bounds, and me

an unplayable lie. We are born
in an open field and then we die;

in the rough, or in the sand, hard
up against the base of a tree, or

underneath an overhanging branch.
In a dark wood is how I won't remember

him, but striding down the fairway,
a bag of woods and irons on his back,

looking for the best approach shot
to the green, hoping for an up-and-in.

A round with him was an education;
on doing your best and playing fair,

on taking each shot as it comes and,
if you have to, on losing well. I want

his death to go to hell and yet, I know
that wouldn't be his way; a handshake

with your opponent, and then, the long
drive home, and calling it a day.

GORDON MEADE

Do Làmh a Chrìosda

Do làmh, a Chrìosda, bi leinn an còmhnaidh;
Ar sìol gu fàs thu, ar gàrradh ròsan;
Ar foghair buan' Thu, ar cruach dhen eòrna –
Nad shaibhlean biomaid aig crìch ar beò-bhith.

Ar n-oiteag chùbhraidh, ar driùchd na Màigh Thu,
Ar cala dìdein an tìmean gàbhaidh,
Ar grunndan iasgaich, ar biadh, ar sàth Thu,
Nad lìontaibh biomaid aig ìre bàis dhuinn.

Nar làithean leanabais biodh d'ainm-sa beò dhuinn,
Nar làithean aosta do ghaol biodh còmh' rinn,
Tro neòil ar dùbh'rachd ar cùrsa treòraich,
Tro shiantan dùr', gu reul-iùil ar dòchais.

Cha chrìoch am bàs dhuinn ach fàs às ùr dhuinn -
O lìon led ghràs sinn, gu bràth bi dlùth dhuinn;
'S nuair thig an t-àm oirnn aig ceann ar n-ùine,
'S e òg-mhìos Mhàigh bhios an àite Dùdlachd.

DÒMHNALL IAIN MACDHÒMHNAILL

Your Hand, O Christ

May your hand, O Christ, be always with us;
Our seed to grow, our garden of roses;
Our autumn harvest, our barley store –
Let us be in your granary at life's end.

You are our fragrant breeze, our May-morn dew,
Our safe harbour in times of danger,
Our fishing ground, our food, our plenty –
Let us be in your nets at time of death.

In childhood may your name live for us,
In old age may your love be with us,
Guide us through our darkest clouds,
Through storms, to our star of hope.

Death is not our end but a new beginning –
Fill us with your grace and stay close forever;
So that when the end of our time comes,
May's young month will replace dark winter.

DONALD JOHN MACDONALD
translation by JOHN CAMPBELL

Praise of a man

He went through a company like a lamplighter –
see the dull minds, one after another,
begin to glow, to shed
a beneficent light.

He went through a company like
a knifegrinder – see the dull minds
scattering sparks of themselves,
becoming razory, becoming useful.

He went through a company
as himself. But now he's one
of the multitudinous company of the dead
where are no individuals.

The beneficent lights dim
but don't vanish. The razory edges
dull, but still cut. He's gone: but you can see
his tracks still, in the snow of the world.

NORMAN MACCAIG

The Bird that was Trapped has Flown

in memoriam Vicky Patterson

The bird that was trapped has flown
The sky that was grey is blue
The bone that was dead has grown
The dream that was dreamed is true
The locked door has been swung wide
The prisoner has been set free
The lips that were sealed have cried
The eye that was blind can see
The tree that was bare is green
The room that was dull is bright
The sheet that was soiled is clean
The dawn that was dark is light
The road that was blocked has no end
The unknown journey is known
The heart that is hurt will mend
The bird that was trapped has flown

JAMES ROBERTSON

The Transmutation

That all should change to ghost and glance and gleam,
And so transmuted stand beyond all change,
And we be poised between the unmoving dream
And the sole moving moment – this is strange

Past all contrivance, word, or image, or sound,
Or silence, to express, that we who fall
Through time's long ruin should weave this phantom
ground
And in its ghostly borders gather all.

There incorruptible the child plays still,
The lover waits beside the trysting tree,
The good hour spans its heaven, and the ill,
Rapt in their silent immortality,

As in commemoration of a day
That having been can never pass away.

EDWIN MUIR

Epitaph on my own Friend

An honest man here lies at rest,
As e'er God with His image blest:
The friend of man, the friend of truth;
The friend of age, and guide of youth:
Few hearts like his, with virtue warm'd,
Few heads with knowledge so inform'd:
If there's another world, he lives in bliss;
If there is none, he made the best of this.

ROBERT BURNS

The Joy of Living

Farewell you Northern hills, you mountains all,
   goodbye;
Moorland and stony ridges, crags and peaks, goodbye.
Glyder Fach farewell, Cul Beig, Scafell, cloud-bearing
   Suilven.
Sun-warmed rock and the cold of Bleaklow's frozen
   sea –
The snow and the wind and the rain on hills and
   mountains.
Days in the sun and the tempered wind and the air
   like wine,
And you drink and you drink till you're drunk on the
   joy of living.

Farewell to you, my love, my time is almost done.
Lie in my arms once more until the darkness comes.
You filled all my days, held the night at bay, dearest
   companion.
Years pass by and are gone with the speed of birds in
   flight,
Our life like the verse of a song heard in the mountains.
Give me your hand then, love, and join your voice
   with mine,
We'll sing of the hurt and the pain and the joy of living.

Farewell to you, my chicks, soon you must fly alone,
Flesh of my flesh, my future life, bone of my bone.
May your wings be strong, may your days be long,
    safe be your journey.
Each of you bears inside of you the gift of love,
May it bring you light and warmth and the pleasure of
    giving;
Eagerly savour each new day and the taste of its mouth,
Never lose sight of the thrill and the joy of living.

Take me to some high place of heather, rock and ling,
Scatter my dust and ashes, feed me to the wind,
So that I will be part of all you see, the air you are
    breathing –
I'll be part of the curlew's cry and the soaring hawk,
The blue milkwort and the sundew hung with
    diamonds;
I'll be riding the gentle wind that blows through your
    hair,
Reminding you how we shared in the joy of living.

EWAN MACCOLL

Salm 23

Is e Dia fhèin as buachaill dhomh,
cha bhi mi ann an dìth.
Bheir e fa-near gun laighinn sìos
air cluainean glas' le sìth:

Is fòs ri taobh nan aibhnichean
thèid seachad sìos gu mall,
Ata e ga mo threòrachadh,
gu mìn rèidh anns gach ball.

Tha 'g aiseag m' anam dhomh air ais:
's a' treòrachadh mo cheum
Air slighean glan' na fìreantachd,
air sgàth dheagh ainmne fhèin.

Seadh, fòs ged ghluaisinn eadhon trìd
ghlinn dorcha sgàil a' bhàis,
Aon olc no urchaid a theachd orm
chan eagal leam 's cha chàs;

Airson gu bheil thu leam a-ghnàth,
do lorg, 's do bhata treun,
Tha iad a' tabhairt comhfhurtachd
is fuasglaidh dhomh am fheum.

Dhomh dheasaich bòrd air beul mo nàmh
le ola dh'ung mo cheann;
Cur thairis tha mo chupan fòs,
aig meud an làin a th' ann.

Ach leanaidh math is tròcair rium,
an cian a bhìos mi beò;
Is còmhnaicheam an àros Dhè,
ri fad mo rè 's mo lò.

Gaelic Metrical Psalm

The 23rd Psalm o King Dauvit

The Lord's my herd, I sall nocht want.
　　Whaur green the gresses grow
sall be my fauld. He caas me aye
　　whaur fresh sweet burnies rowe.

He gars my saul be blyth aince mair
　　that wandert was frae hame,
and leads me on the straucht smaa gait
　　for sake o His ain name.

Tho I suld gang the glen o mirk
　　I'ld grue for nae mischance,
Thou bydes wi me, Thy kent and cruik
　　maks aye my sustenance.

Thou spreids ane brod and gies me meat
　　whaur aa my faes may view,
Thou sains my heid wi ulyie owre
　　and pours my cogie fou.

Nou seil and kindliness sall gae
　　throu aa my days wi me,
and I sall wone in God's ain hous
　　at hame eternallie.

frae the Hebrew
DOUGLAS YOUNG

herd	*shepherd*
fauld	*fold*
caas	*drives*
rowe	*roll*
gars	*makes*
straucht smaa gait	*straight narrow track*
mirk	*darkness*
grue	*feel a chill of horror*
kent and cruik	*shepherd's pole and crook*
brod	*board, table*
meat	*food*
faes	*enemies*
sains	*blesses*
ulyie	*oil*
cogie	*bowl*
seil	*blessing*
wone	*dwell*

Walking with You

Remember the times we walked the hill
and the wiry yellow tormentil
sprang back as our boots passed,
those days when the air was crisp
and full of larks spinning to dark dots
at the top of their flight,
and music tumbled down on us.

Now death has crossed your hill,
and you are the trodden tormentil
lifting your golden face to a different sky.
You are the lark flown higher than I can see,
your song permeates my air
and I breathe you while I wait for winter
when your spirit will enter the mountain hare,
outrunning every shadow.

PAULA JENNINGS

Fall

after Rilke

The leaves are falling, falling from trees
in dying gardens far above us; as if their slow
free-fall was the sky declining.

And tonight, this heavy earth is falling away
from all the other stars, drawing into silence.

We are all falling now. My hand, my heart,
stall and drift in darkness, see-sawing down.

And we still believe there is one who sifts and holds
the leaves, the lives, of all those softly falling.

ROBIN ROBERTSON

Consolation

Though he that ever kind and true
Kept stoutly step by step with you
Your whole long gusty lifetime through,
　　Be gone awhile before,
Be now a moment gone before,
Yet, doubt not, soon the seasons shall restore
　　Your friend to you.

He has but turned a corner. Still
He pushes on with right good will,
Through mire and marsh, by heugh and hill,
　　That self-same arduous way,
That self-same upland, hopeful way
That you and he through many a doubtful day
　　Attempted still.

He is not dead, this friend – not dead,
But in the path we mortals tread
Got some few trifling steps ahead
　　And nearer to the end;
So that you too, once past the bend,
Shall meet again, as face to face, this friend
　　You fancy dead.

Push gaily on, strong heart! The while
You travel forward mile by mile,
He loiters with a backward smile
    Till you can overtake,
And strains his eyes to search his wake,
Or whistling, as he sees you through the brake,
    Waits on a stile.

ROBERT LOUIS STEVENSON

heugh   *cliff*
brake   *thicket*

The Brig

I whiles gang tae the brig-side
　　That's past the brier tree
Alang the road when the licht is wide
　　O'er Angus and the sea.

In by the dyke yon brier grows
　　Wi' leaf an' thorn its lane
And the spunk o' flame o' the brier rose
　　Burns saft agin' the stane.

And whiles a step treids on by me,
　　I mauna hear its fa',
But atween the brig an' the brier tree
　　There gangs na' ane, but twa.

Oot o'er yon sea, through war and strife
　　Ye tak yer road nae mair,
For ye've crossed the brig to the fields o' life
　　And ye walk for ever there.

I trayvel to the brig-side
　　Whaur ilka road maun cease,
My weary war may be lang tae bide
　　And you hae won tae peace.

There's ne'er a nicht but turns tae day,
    Nor a load that's niver cast;
And there's nae wind cries on the winter brae
    But it spends itsel' at last.

O you that niver failed me yet,
    Gin aince my step ye hear,
Come to yon brig atween us set
    And bide till I win near!

Oh weel, aye weel ye'll ken my treid,
    Ye'll seek nae word nor sign,
An' I'll no can fail at yon Brig o' Dreid
    For yer hand will be in mine.

VIOLET JACOB

brig	*bridge*
whiles	*sometimes*
dyke	*ditch*
its lane	*on its own*
spunk	*glimmer*
mauna	*must not*

An t-Aingheal Dìona

Aingil Dhè a fhuair mo chùram
Bho Athair cùmh na tròcaireachd,
Ciobaireachd caon crò nan naomh
Dhèanamh dha mo thaobh a-nochd;

Fuad uam gach buar is cunnart
Cuairt mi air cuan na dòbhachd,
Anns a' chunglait, chaimleit, chumhan,
Cùm mo churach fèin an-còmhnàidh.

Bi na do lasair lèith romham,
Bi na do rèil iùil tharam,
Bi na do rod rèidh fotham,
Is na do chìobair caomh mo dheoghann,
An-diugh, a-nochd agus gu suthann.

Tha mi sgìth is mi air m' aineol,
Treòraich mi do thìr nan aingeal;
Leam is tìm a bhi dol dachaigh
Do chùirt Chrìost, do shìth nam flathas.

from *Carmina Gadelica*

The Guardian Angel

O Angel of God whom the gentle Father
Of mercy has charged with my care
To undertake my gentle shepherding
To the fold of the saints tonight;

Drive me from every temptation and danger,
Surround me on the sea of unrighteousness,
And in the narrows, crooks, and straits,
Keep thou my coracle, keep it always.

Be thou a bright flame before me,
Be thou a guiding star above me,
Be thou a smooth path below me,
And be a kindly shepherd behind me,
Today, tonight, and forever.

I am tired and I a stranger,
Lead thou me to the land of angels;
For me it is time to go home
To the court of Christ, to the peace of heaven.

adapted from the translation by ALEXANDER CARMICHAEL

Metamorphosis

If, when the story ends, we are transformed
to something else: new memories and tastes
arriving from the dark and suddenly
familiar, like the strangers in a dream,

new eyes to see the world, another light
unfolding in another type of brain,
a foreign tongue for mimicry or song,
frogskin or petals, swansdown or living fur,

if we return to what we cannot lose
as anything at all, let us be moths
and wander in the certainties of grass
and buttercups, unsure of what we are,
but ready, for as long as time allows,
to fill the meadows with a new becoming.

JOHN BURNSIDE

Song

End is in beginning;
And in beginning end:
Death is not loss, nor life winning;
But each and to each is friend.

The hands which give are taking;
And the hands which take bestow:
Always the bough is breaking
Heavy with fruit or snow.

WILLIAM SOUTAR

Departure and Departure and . . .

Someone is waving a white handkerchief
from the train as it pulls out with a white
plume from the station and rumbles its way
to somewhere that does not matter. But
it will pass the white sands and the broad sea
that I have watched under the sun and moon
in the stop of time in my childhood as I am
now there again and waiting for the white
handkerchief. I shall not see her again
but the waters rise and fall and the horizon
is firm. You who have not seen that line
hold the brimming sea to the round earth
cannot know this pain and sweetness of departure.

GEORGE BRUCE

The Flyting o' Life and Daith

Quo life, the warld is mine.
The floo'ers and trees, they're a' my ain.
I am the day, and the sunshine
Quo life, the warld is mine.

Quo daith, the warld is mine.
Your lugs are deef, your een are blin
Your floo'ers maun dwine in my bitter win'
Quo daith, the warld is mine.

Quo life, the warld is mine.
I hae saft win's, an' healin' rain,
Aipples I hae, an' breid an' wine
Quo life, the warld is mine.

Quo daith, the warld is mine.
Whit sterts in dreid, gangs doon in pain
Bairns wantin' breid are makin' mane
Quo daith, the warld is mine.

Quo life, the warld is mine.
Your deidly wark, I ken it fine
There's maet on earth for ilka wean
Quo life, the warld is mine.

Quo daith, the warld is mine.
Your silly sheaves crine in my fire

58   My worm keeks in your barn and byre
      Quo daith, the warld is mine.

      Quo life, the warld is mine.
      Dule on your een! Ae galliard hert
      Can ban tae hell your blackest airt
      Quo life, the warld is mine.

      Quo daith, the warld is mine.
      Your rantin' hert, in duddies braw,
      He winna lowp my preeson wa'
      Quo daith, the warld is mine.

      Quo life, the warld is mine.
      Though ye bigg preesons o' marble stane
      Hert's luve ye cannae preeson in
      Quo life, the world is mine.

      Quo daith, the warld is mine.
      I hae dug a grave, I hae dug it deep,
      For war an' the pest will gar ye sleep.
      Quo daith, the warld is mine.

      Quo life, the warld is mine.
      An open grave is a furrow syne.
      Ye'll no keep my seed frae fa'in in.
      Quo life, the warld is mine.

      HAMISH HENDERSON

flyting	*disputation*
lugs	*ears*
maun dwine	*must fade*
maet	*food*
ilka wean	*each child*
crine	*shrivel*
dule	*misery*
ae galliard hert	*one gallant heart*
ban	*curse*
duddies braw	*glad rags*
lowp	*leap over*
bigg	*build*
gar	*make*
syne	*next, thereafter*

Hamewith

En ma fin est mon commencement.

— Marie Stuart

Man at the end
Til the womb wends,
Fisher til sea,
Hunter to hill,
Miner the pit seeks,
Sodjer the bield.

As bairn on breist
Seeks his first need
Makar his thocht prees,
Doer his deed,
Sanct his peace
And sinner remeid.

Man in dust is lain
And exile wins hame.

SYDNEY GOODSIR SMITH

til	*to*	prees	*tries out*
sodjer	*soldier*	sanct	*saint*
bield	*shelter*	wins hame	*comes home*
makar	*poet*		

WILLIAM ALEXANDER (c.1567–1640), first Earl of Stirling, was born at Menstrie Castle and became tutor to Henry, son of James VI. He followed the court to London, and was knighted in 1609. He was a poet, composer and playwright; his output includes songs and an epic poem as well as his verse tragedies.

GEORGE MACKAY BROWN (1921–1996) Apart from some years in the 1950s studying at Newbattle College and at Edinburgh University, George Mackay Brown rarely left his native Orkney. His poems and stories are centred in the history and culture of the island, and reflect his concern with preserving traditions and ritual. He received an OBE in 1974, and was made a fellow of the Royal Society of Literature in 1977. The *Collected Poems* were published by John Murray in 2005.

GEORGE BRUCE (1909–2002) was born and brought up in Fraserburgh, and the lean landscape and the sea of the North-East are mirrored in his sparse, telling poems. He was a producer with BBC radio for thirty years, in Aberdeen and Edinburgh. *Today Tomorrow: the Collected Poems of George Bruce 1933–2000* was published by Polygon in 2001, but he kept writing up until his death at the age of 92, and *Through the Letterbox*, a collaboration with artist Elizabeth Blackadder, appeared in 2003.

ROBERT BURNS (1759–1796) is known and loved as Scotland's national bard. He was born in Ayrshire, the son of a farmer, and achieved his first success with the publication of *Poems, Chiefly in the Scottish Dialect* in 1786. His poems are translated into many languages; he himself was at home writing in English or Scots, and in many different verse forms. Burns served Scotland well both as poet and as a dedicated collector of the country's ballads and song.

JOHN BURNSIDE (b.1955) was born in Dunfermline. His first collection of poetry, *The Hoop*, was published in 1988 and won a Scottish Arts Council Book Award; since then there have been nine more books of poetry, the latest being *The Good Neighbour* (Jonathan Cape, 2005). *The Asylum Dance* (2000) was winner of the Whitbread Poetry Award. Also a short-story writer and novelist, John Burnside lives in Fife, and teaches at the University of St Andrews.

JOHN CAMPBELL is from South Uist but now lives in Barra where he was headmaster of Castlebay Secondary School for 27 years, after teaching Gaelic in Glasgow. He adjudicates at the Mod, and occasionally presents programmes on Gaelic television.

ALEXANDER CARMICHAEL (1832–1912) gathered together between 1855 and 1899, largely from the Western Isles, a magnificent collection of Gaelic lore which was published as *Carmina Gadelica* (in five volumes, 1900–1954). The *Carmina* is mostly in the form of verse, with prayers, blessings, and work songs, accompanied by extensive notes and Carmichael's translations into English.

R. L. COOK (1921–2004) was born and educated in Edinburgh, and lived there until the 1970s, after service in the Navy during the war and afterwards. From the 1950s onwards he was widely published in magazines in Scotland and abroad, and his poetry was collected in a series of eight books, the last being *Waiting for the End* (The Lomond Press, 2001).

CHRISTINE DE LUCA (b.1947) was born and brought up in Shetland. Now living in Edinburgh, she writes in both Shetland dialect and English, and the Shetland Library has published three books of her poetry, the most recent being *Plain Song* (2002). Her poems have been translated into several languages, and published in both national and international magazines; she is currently working on story books and CDs for children in Shetlandic.

HAMISH HENDERSON (1919–2002) Poet, songwriter and folklorist Hamish Henderson was born in Blairgowrie, Perthshire. He worked for the School of Scottish Studies of Edinburgh University from the 1950s as a field researcher and collector of traditional songs, and was himself a leading figure of the Scottish folk revival. His experience of war in North Africa led to the publication of *Elegies for the Dead in Cyrenaica* (John Lehmann, 1948); his *Collected Poems and Songs* were published by Curly Snake in 2000.

VIOLET JACOB (1863–1946) was born near Montrose, and lived in India and England after marriage to a British army officer, returning to Angus after her husband's death. She wrote fiction and poetry in English, but her best poetry was written in Scots, with a true ear for the dialect of her native country, pre-dating the upsurge of interest in Scots of the Scottish Rennaissance with her collections *Songs of Angus* (1915, 1918). Her only son was killed at the Battle of the Somme in 1916.

PAULA JENNINGS (b.1950) is a teacher of creative writing in Edinburgh. She has received SAC bursaries and, in 2003, a Hawthornden Writing Fellowship. Her poems have appeared in a number of literary magazines and anthologies, and her collection *Singing Lucifer* was published by Onlywomen Press in 2002.

NORMAN MACCAIG (1910–1996) was born in Edinburgh, where he worked for many years as a primary school teacher. From *Riding Lights* in 1955 to *Voice Over* in 1988 he published fourteen collections of poetry. He was appointed Fellow in Creative Writing at Edinburgh in 1967, and in 1970 he became a Reader in poetry at the University of Stirling. For most of his life, MacCaig divided his time between Edinburgh and Assynt in the north-west Highlands: the landscape of the latter in particular is a recurring theme of his poetry. *Poems of Norman MacCaig* was published by Polygon in 2005.

EWAN MACCOLL (1915–1989) Born Jimmie Miller in Lancashire, his mother was from Perthshire, and he grew up steeped in Scottish songs and ballads. A singer, songwriter and playwright, he founded Theatre Workshop in the 1940s, and was a leading figure in the folksong revival of the 1950s; with his wife Peggy Seeger he pioneered the radio-ballad documentaries broadcast by the BBC.

DONALD JOHN MACDONALD / DÒMHNALL IAIN MACDHÒMHNAILL (1919–1986) Born in South Uist, into a family who kept up the tradition of storytelling and oral poetry, Donald John evolved a more modern idiom for writing his own poetry. He spent the years 1940–45 as a prisoner of war in Germany; the book *Fo Sgàil a' Swastika / Under the Shadow of the Swastika* (Acair, 2000) is an account of these years. His poetry is collected in *Chì Mi: bàrdachd Dhòmhnaill Iain Dhonnchaidh / I See: the poetry of Donald John MacDonald* (Birlinn, 1998).

GORDON MEADE (b.1957) lives in Fife. He has been the Creative Writing Fellow at Duncan of Jordanstone College of Art /Writer in Residence for Dundee District Libraries, and the Creative Writing Tutor for East Lothian's WIRED Out of School Hours project. His poetry is available in pamphlet form, and his most recent full-length publication is *A Man At Sea* (diehard press, 2004).

EDWIN MORGAN (b. 1920) was born in Glasgow and has lived there all his life, except for service with the RAMC in the Middle East during the Second World War. His poetry is grounded in the city, though he is also a prolific translator from many languages. He retired from Glasgow University as titular Professor of English in 1980, serving as Glasgow's first Poet Laureate 1999–2002. In February 2004 he became the first 'Scots Makar', in effect Scotland's poet laureate. His *Collected Poems* (Carcanet, 1990) and *Collected Translations* (Carcanet, 1996) have been succeeded by several volumes of poetry, including *Cathures* (Carcanet, 2002) and *Love and a life* (Mariscat, 2003).

EDWIN MUIR (1887–1959) was born in Orkney, but moved to Glasgow with his family when he was fourteen. His poetic vision is strongly influenced by a longing for lost Edens and lost childhood, as well as his apocalyptic sense of war and its aftermath. An influential critic as well as poet, he published seven volumes of poetry, collected together in *The Complete Poems of Edwin Muir* (Faber, 1991).

JANET PAISLEY (b.1948) grew up in central Scotland where she still lives. Her publications include five collections of poetry, the most recent being *Ye Cannae Win*, (Chapman, 2000); two of short stories; plays for theatre and radio; TV drama, and film. Her work has been widely translated. 'Mountain Thyme' was written to mark her mother's death and first appeared in *Reading the Bones* (Canongate, 1999).

DAVID PURVES (b. 1924) was born in Selkirk, took his degrees at Edinburgh University, and followed a career as an agricultural biochemist. Dr Purves has long been an activist in the cause of the Scots language, editing the magazine *Lallans* 1987–1995. He is a prolific translator into Scots of ancient Chinese and other poetry, and has written plays in Scots, as well as his own poetry, which was published in *Hert's Bluid* (Chapman, 1995).

KATHLEEN RAINE (1908–2003) was half Scottish; the landscape of the Highlands and that of her childhood Northumbria find a place in her poetry, which largely explores the relationship between man and nature, and man and the sacred. She was a scholar and critic, the founder of *Temenos* review and the Temenos Academy, and author of numerous books of poetry; the *Collected Poems* was published by Golgonooza Press in 2000. Kathleen Raine received the Queen's Gold Medal for Poetry in 1992, and both the CBE and the Commandeur de L'Ordre des Arts et des Lettres in 2000.

JAMES ROBERTSON (b.1958) is a poet, novelist, and editor. His poetry includes *I Dream of Alfred Hitchcock*, (Kettillonia, 1999) and Scots versions of Baudelaire in *Fae the Flouers o Evil* (Kettillonia, 2001). He compiled a new edition of Robert Fergusson's selected poems in 2000, marking the 250th anniversary of the poet's birth, and is general editor of the Scots language imprint Itchy Coo. His second novel, *Joseph Knight* (2003), won both the Saltire and the Scottish Arts Council Book of the Year awards. In November 2004 he was the first Writer in Residence at the Scottish Parliament.

ROBIN ROBERTSON (b.1955) was born in Scotland. He has spent over twenty years working in publishing, currently at Jonathan Cape. His own poetry collections are *A Painted Field*

(Picador, 1997), which won several prizes, including the Saltire Society Scottish First Book of the Year award, and *Slow Air*, (Picador, 2002). In 2004 he received the E.M. Forster Award from the American Academy of Arts and Letters.

IAIN CRICHTON SMITH / IAIN MAC A' GOBHAINN (1928–1998) was raised on the island of Lewis, and spent most of his life as a schoolteacher in Glasgow and Oban, receiving an OBE in 1980. From *The Long River* (Macdonald, 1955) to *A Country for Old Men* (Carcanet, 2000), he was a prolific writer in both English and Gaelic, of poetry and fiction; a sense of exile is at the heart of his work. His view of Scotland's culture, small communities and religion was never romantic, but he had a keen eye for small delights and a strong sense of wonder.

SYDNEY GOODSIR SMITH (1915–1975) was half Scottish; born in New Zealand in 1915, he was educated in England, and studied at Edinburgh and Oxford Universities. His interest in medieval Scots led him to adopt Scots for his own work; his long love poem, 'Under the Eildon Tree' shows his mastery of the language. He also wrote a novel, *Carotid Cornucopius* (1947); his play *The Wallace* was performed at the Edinburgh Festival of 1960; the poetry is gathered in *Collected Poems 1941–1975* (John Calder, 1975).

WILLIAM SOUTAR (1898–1943) One of the poets of the Scottish Renaissance, Soutar started to write in Scots for both adults and children in the 1920s. Having contracted an illness while in the Navy during the First World War which led to ossification of the spine, he was confined to bed for the last thirteen years of his life; this did not diminish the humour and power of his poetry. His literary output also included diaries and journals; *Into a Room: selected poems of William Soutar* (Argyll Publishing, 2000) is the most recent edition of his poetry.

ROBERT LOUIS STEVENSON (1850–1894), author of the well-loved tales *Treasure Island* and *Kidnapped*, was also a poet. His best-known collection is *A Child's Garden of Verses*, but Stevenson also wrote much lyric poetry, and a range of lively verse in Scots. He was born in Edinburgh, but – for the sake of his health – travelled and lived abroad, and is buried in Samoa. The most recent full edition of his poetry is *The Collected Poetry of Robert Louis Stevenson*, edited by Roger C. Lewis (Edinburgh University Press, 2003).

GAEL TURNBULL (1928–2004) was a medical practitioner in Britain, America and Canada, and returned to live in Edinburgh, where he was born. His work ranged from prose poetry and collage poems to his inventive 'poem-objects', but all express a 'delight in language and in the possibilities of utterance'. His published poetry is collected in *A Gathering of Poems 1950–1980* (Anvil, 1983), *For Whose Delight* (Mariscat, 1995), *Might a Shape of Words* (Mariscat, 2000), and many smaller publications.

HAMISH WHYTE (b.1947) is a poet, publisher, editor, and former librarian. He has edited several anthologies of Scottish poetry, including *Mungo's Tongues: Glasgow Poems 1630–1990* (Mainstream, 1993) and *20 Best Scottish Poems 2003–4* (SPL online, 2004). He contributes to current poetry publishing in Scotland with his Mariscat Press, and is an Honorary Research Fellow at the Department of Scottish Literature, University of Glasgow.

DOUGLAS YOUNG (1913–1973) poet and essayist, was a 'colourful and memorable figure' of the Scottish Renaissance. He studied at St Andrews and Oxford, taught at Aberdeen University, became a leading member of the young Scottish National Party, and was imprisoned for refusing conscription in 1942 (where he completed *Auntran Blads*, his first book of poems). He was a master of translation into Scots, and had an international reputation as a scholar of Greek, teaching classics in North America from the 1960s until his death.